eart Mandalas
Coloring Book

Marty Noble

DOVER PUBLICATIONS, INC.
Mineola, New York

NOTE

Combine hearts and mandalas, and the result is an amazing array of ready-to-color images! In addition to dozens of hearts of various sizes, you'll find intricate borders, charming cupids, and images from nature, such as strawberries, bees, flowers, and birds. All of the designs radiate into symmetrically balanced mandalas. Experience a touch of romance as you color page after page of pleasing patterns.

Bibliographical Note
Heart Mandalas Coloring Book is a new work, first published by Dover Publications, Inc., in 2013.

International Standard Book Number
ISBN-13: 978-0-486-49219-3
ISBN-10: 0-486-49219-2

Manufactured in the United States by Courier Corporation
49219201   2013
www.doverpublications.com